Remanso

THE REVEALING REALITY OF
A CUBAN-AMERICAN WOMAN

SARAH TRIANA

iUniverse, Inc.
New York   Bloomington

Remanso
The Revealing Reality of a Cuban-American Woman

iUniverse books may be ordered through booksellers or by contacting:

iUniverse
1663 Liberty Drive
Bloomington, IN 47403
www.iuniverse.com
1-800-Authors (1-800-288-4677)

Because of the dynamic nature of the Internet, any Web addresses or links contained in this book may have changed since publication and may no longer be valid. The views expressed in this work are solely those of the author and do not necessarily reflect the views of the publisher, and the publisher hereby disclaims any responsibility for them.

ISBN: 978-1-4502-3129-9 (sc)
ISBN: 978-1-4502-3128-2 (dj)
ISBN: 978-1-4502-3130-5 (ebook)

Printed in the United States of America

iUniverse rev. date: 05/11/2010

This book is dedicated to the memory of my mother and those in need of encouragement and hope.

**** **** ****

*Love is
hope and joy.
Love is
the light of our lives.
Love is
a precious gift.*

Sarah Triana, 1971

**** **** ****

Contents

Introduction

Some people go trough life feeling unhappy even though they are lucky enough to have been blessed with what most people would consider a "good life". Others are generally happy even after having experienced disappointments. Then, there are those who feel as if they have lived three or four lives through the course of just one life. I am one of those people.

I have lived through ordinary days in which I have felt worse than I have during my most devastating days. I am aware that how you feel within has nothing to do with what is going on "outside." Therefore, we must remain very conscious of what goes on "inside" of us because the key dwells within.

As a woman in my early fifties, I have become wiser than I was in my younger years. Although I am far from perfect, one thing that I am proud of in this life is my ability to have made it through probably not just one, but at least "three" of what most people would consider their "most traumatic experiences." I also know that I could not have done it without the help of God and a few nice people along the way.

As I get older, I have made it my business to reach out to those in need of encouragement. I believe that there are many ordinary people who consider committing suicide from time to time. I also know that there are some who choose to take drugs—and not necessarily for medical reasons. It is my ultimate goal in this life to make these people realize that, if God continues to give us a new day, it is because there is always hope—no matter how hard life seems at times.

The most important reason why I am sitting here writing today is because I hope, through these pages, to help at least one person in need of encouragement and hope. It would be most gratifying to me to accomplish that.

To all of you who are about to read what I am about to tell you, may I remind you that the spirit of God lives within all of us.

CHAPTER I
The Sad News

S HE WAS the best. In my world, no other mother could even come close when compared to mine. She had such devotion and so much love. She was always singing and was always there for me. She used to call me "*mi remanso de paz*" (my peaceful refuge). I was too young to comprehend the meaning of "peace." However, she never knew that the peace that radiated from me was generated by her. She was, after all, the peaceful refuge, not me. I realized this after she was gone as the peace left with her.

December 31, 1965, was the last New Year's Eve that I spent with my mother. She was not well. I remember that she was in so much pain that she could barely walk. However, she still managed to fill up a bucket with water at midnight and proceeded to dump the water out the front door in hopes of getting rid of any bad luck. It had been our family tradition back in Cuba. It was also our tradition to eat twelve grapes along with the champagne at midnight. It was just us that New Year's Eve. My father was working as a musician at the hotel as usual. My sister had gone to a party with my grandmother and a friend. I still remember my mother sitting across from me that night.

It was strange to feel the way I did while she was in the hospital. It was horrifying for me to find out that she was going to leave me before she left. The strange man's voice I heard in the night two days prior to her death told me that she was going to die, but no one believed me. No one understood why I cried for no reason at all prior to her death. It took many years for me to learn to understand that the voice was part of the plan, the higher power, and the divine force. From that moment on, it started to evolve within me and somehow turned me into who I am today.

I opened my eyes early that morning and saw my father sitting on a stool in our bedroom. My sister was thirteen and I was nine years old.

He simply said, "Your mother died last night."

It is funny how the brain of a nine-year-old works. I thought that she had died, but that she would be coming back. After all, he only said that she had died. I waited for days for her face to come into my room, but she was gone and there was no one to explain to me why she wasn't coming back. What was so complicated about "death" that did not allow someone to come back to say good-bye?

I still remember waiting at the funeral home by the side of the coffin for her eyes to open. She had the most beautiful green eyes and they were starting to open up after so many hours. I remember the pouring rain while she was being buried the next day. I recall thinking that there had to be a reason for it to be raining so hard during those painful moments. I went home that day convinced, at least for the moment, that she wasn't going to wake up—not just yet.

It took months, but finally I stopped waiting for her to return. Instead, I learned to feel her presence within my surroundings and it is that presence that has been with me all my life.

I have never been able to recover from the pain of losing my mother at such young age. Nevertheless, I learned what only one who loses someone so close learns: love remains and memories do last a lifetime. They help us cope with the loss if we allow ourselves to do so by having faith and by being aware that there is a divine power that somehow connects us all.

I am convinced that you have to feel the pain in order to come close to understanding what it is like to lose someone that you love and trust. Unfortunately, there is no other way to even come close to understanding that hopeless feeling. The loss of someone I loved and betrayal are two things I had to learn to deal with at a very young age. In addition, while I do not wish these experiences on anyone, I believe that, unless you experience the hurt, you will go through life unaware of how lucky you really are when you are surrounded by people that love you and that you love and trust in return.

I learned that in order to go on I sometimes would have to transport myself to my own peaceful refuge. I learned to listen, observe, and pray. Miraculously, my pain transformed into something that I could handle. I realized at an early age that, while there is tomorrow, there is always hope.

CHAPTER II
Maria

IRECENTLY learned what I believe to be the true story about my grandmother Maria. She was beautiful, sweet, and caring. My mother died in her arms.

She was young and gorgeous when she met my grandfather, Juan Jose. They were both very young. My grandfather was a barber. They married and had a total of five children. However, living with Juan Jose was not easy.

By the time my mother was about eight or nine years old, my grandmother's marriage had already started to deteriorate. My mother and her sister, along with their oldest brother, were being forced to grow up in a very stressful, traumatic environment. My grandfather—who was eventually diagnosed as schizophrenic in his eighties after he finally agreed to be examined by a psychiatrist—would have violent outbursts that would make people's lives around him intolerable. However, in 1936, having affairs seemed to be easier and more socially acceptable than getting a divorce.

Julio was the name of the man who changed Maria's life. He

was a policeman. He was unhappily married and had recently separated from his wife. They lived in the same neighborhood, but no one really knows how they met. They used to meet at a park. Maria told the children, including my uncle who liked Julio very much, that Julio was their cousin. They would spend time together at the park. The children enjoyed Julio's company and would look forward to spending time together. This went on for quite some time.

It was after a very big argument that my grandmother decided to leave Juan Jose. She took the girls with her (my mother and my aunt) and ran away with Julio. Julio had rented two adjoining rooms at a nearby hotel. Their plan was to leave my uncle with my grandfather and for Maria to take the two girls, at least for the moment. However, this would turn out to be a decision that left my uncle scarred for life as he felt totally abandoned.

Still, as a woman in that predicament, how do you deal with such a situation when your life has become unbearable? Maria felt that it was in her son's best interest for him to remain with his father—especially at twelve or thirteen years of age. Ultimately, leaving my uncle with his father turned out to not be such a good idea.

Just as Maria and Julio were getting ready to move into a nice little house with the girls, Juan Jose visited Julio with a loaded gun. A neighbor had told him where to find them. He said that he was going to kill my grandmother if she did not return the girls to him.

It was clear that my grandfather Juan Jose loved my grandmother Maria very much and that he had the best interests of the children at heart. While he felt a great deal of love for my grandmother, he was also an incredibly dangerous man capable of committing murder.

Shortly after Juan Jose took the girls away, Maria made the hardest and saddest decision of her entire life. She decided to go back to him. She realized that she could not live without her children. The girls never got to see their room at their new house. They never got to see the skates that they had been asking for, which Julio had bought for them as a surprise. My aunt would talk about the skates from time to time as if she was somewhat disappointed that their plans had never worked out.

One morning, my grandfather was sitting at the courthouse with my mother and my aunt by his side. He was waiting for his case to be heard when a man said, "Look! That has to be the most beautiful woman I have ever seen." He was referring to my grandmother who was entering the courtroom (not realizing that my grandfather was her husband). My grandfather replied, "It is because of that woman that I am here today." The man just walked away rather confused.

Eventually, Juan Jose succeeded in his efforts to regain control of his family. Was it love for my grandmother that made him act like a madman or was it just an incredible obsession and need to control her? What about my grandmother? Did she continue living or merely existing after that? She was now pregnant with her fourth child. Only time would tell.

Juan Jose had always been a very good provider. After my grandmother returned home, he continued to provide for his family in the same consistent manner as he had always done. This made it easier for my grandmother to cope.

However, the arguments between Maria and Juan Jose escalated. On several occasions, my mother and aunt witnessed him going insane and pointing a loaded gun at my grandmother. He continued to abuse my grandmother—not only physically, but also mentally—for many years. It would appear that wanting Maria back was not really his plan after all. His ultimate plan was revenge.

Approximately two years after my mother's little sister was born, my grandmother received another surprise. My grandfather announced that he had a son with another woman. He went on to explain to my grandmother how the baby's mother had just died from tuberculosis and how he was going to end up in an orphanage unless he did something about it.

My grandmother was a very sweet and loving woman. She loved children and she was very patient and caring. Therefore, she agreed to adopt the baby boy who she would end up raising as her own. My mother eventually became very attached to her little brother. She used to take care of him all the time since she was much older. Ultimately, they became very close.

My sweet grandmother certainly paid a very high price for having found love in her life. She was like an angel with clipped wings. Her children loved her, but to some extent resented her at the same time. She managed to survive years of abuse from my grandfather. No one really understood her, although it is said that my grandfather's sisters always sided with Maria.

Once the kids were grown up, my grandmother managed to put some distance between her and my grandfather. She moved in with my uncle who had never married and my aunt who was still single at the time.

Thinking about my grandmother's life makes me realize how hard my mother's childhood was. It also makes it clear that growing up in such despair is what taught her to recognize and appreciate the happy moments. Perhaps that is how she learned to live her life to the fullest every day until she died at the age of thirty-eight.

I was fortunate to have my grandmother tell me stories about my mother. She was the best grandmother in the world to me. It was amazing that she still had energy and patience left to spend so much quality time with my sister and me.

After my mother died, she did her best to try to help us. However, it was hard dealing with my father. My paternal grandmother had already moved into our house and felt that there was no need for her to be there. Still, she would take a bus and would come to see us whenever she could. My mother's death really affected her, but she still found the strength to go on. She eventually came to the United States in 1969 and continued to live with my aunt and her family until she died in 1988.

CHAPTER III
The Dead Years

GROWING UP without a mother is not easy when you're nine years old. I refused to accept that she was gone. I remember feeling and acting as if I was on autopilot for six months after she died. When I realized that she wasn't coming back, my whole body went numb and my brain froze. I had been in denial the entire time.

I attempted to get affection from my father. Until my mother died, he had always been very affectionate with me. I clearly remember the day I went by his office in our house. He slammed the door as I was passing by because (as I learned later) I reminded him of my mother in some strange way.

I can still feel the wind hitting my face as I rode the swings at the park across from my house. Sometimes, I remember swinging so high that it felt as if I could touch the sky. I would imagine my mother watching me from the park bench as she used to do many afternoons while she was alive.

I found it very hard to cope—especially after having a mother who adored me and always showed her affection by hugging me and kissing me. The hugs were gone and, although I could still feel her sometimes, my life became empty.

My mother loved music and she always encouraged us to sing, dance, and play the piano. I can still remember her singing all the time. She had a beautiful voice. She recorded a record that I believe my father burned during a rage after she died. She would volunteer to sing at hospitals. Unfortunately, the piano and flamenco dancing lessons stopped immediately after her death.

My father ended up being hospitalized after several electric shock treatments failed to improve his condition and this did not help the situation at all. It was during that time that my paternal grandmother's face became a permanent fixture in our house. I clearly remember resenting her just for being there.

Unfortunately for me, I was a witness to many fights that my mother and my grandmother had through the years. My mother and grandmother had known each other since my mother was a little girl. Consequently, my grandmother probably found it hard to find a common ground in which to treat my mother.

Although my grandmother had rented an apartment located near her job in Habana, she was at my house quite often. My father had built a master bedroom just for her when he had our house built. She used to come over unexpectedly after work sometimes and she was there most weekends. Although I have to admit that it was sometimes nice having her around, my mother ultimately had no privacy. Undoubtedly, my father was very much spoiled by my grandmother and that is what most of their fights were about. Their fights were ugly, but not uglier than any other fight I've witnessed. As a child, been forced to listen to the ruthless words that they yelled at each other, it felt like thorns were going right through my scalp.

The biggest fight transpired only a few months or maybe even weeks before my mother died. I still remember my grandmother kneeling before the enormous picture of the Sacred Heart located just outside my father's office as she and my mother were at it back and forth. She said these words in Spanish as she knelt down, *"Castigala porque ella es mala!"*— (Punish her because she is bad).

Those words stayed with me until my grandmother died at the age of ninety-four. Although my grandmother always knew that I had been a witness to this horrible act, she never brought up the incident. Therefore, we never spoke about it. Having my grandmother take care of us on a full-time basis after my father was hospitalized wasn't easy for me either.

Being raised by a grandmother that I resented with all my heart and who also favored my older sister was very difficult. Yet, deep down, I still loved her—especially as the years went by. I also witnessed her sacrificing her own life to take care of us. However, at that moment, I did not want her near me.

The years right after my mother died were the hardest of my life. I learned to refer to them as the "dead years." They were years of total darkness, where only the presence of God himself within me—along with the memory of my mother—managed to push me forward and ultimately helped me to see the light at the end of a dark, long tunnel.

How can anyone possibly know what it feels like to live in total darkness after having lost all hope? The only way is to experience it. There is no way to describe the pain. I remember there were no drugs. There were no psychologists. There was no one to turn to. Yet, I learned to survive. Strangely,

I've occasionally had to recall and find strength from those moments.

It would seem that the power from within, without the influence of any drugs or even another person, is what has always brought me closer to God and his power.

CHAPTER IV
The Transition

AFTER SURVIVING without my father and mother for about a year, I endured another traumatic time in my life. I will simply refer to her as the stepmother.

I remember the day my father took my sister and I to meet his girlfriend. Apparently, he had met her shortly after he got out of the mental institution where he had remained for almost a year. We never found out exactly how they met. Instead, we found out the hard way how people can manipulate and take advantage of those who are vulnerable.

Going into the apartment where she lived with her parents and her daughter and son was a very strange experience. Her father seemed to be a spiritual authority of some sort and was dressed entirely in white. We even got a glance of his temple where he kept glasses filled with water and some strange religious artifacts. Her mother seemed nice, although very quiet. I don't remember meeting her children that day.

While we were waiting for the bus to go back home, my father announced that he was marrying his girlfriend. My sister who is four years older than I am started arguing with my father. He was firm, loud, and clear when he said that there was no turning back and that he was going through with his plans. I was only eleven years old and was too confused by everything that had happened to even begin to comprehend what that meant to our world. It wasn't long before I realized that our lives were not ours anymore.

I still remember the day my stepmother made us fill up buckets with soap and water and literally forced us to clean the walls of our home, my mother's home, "to get rid of her smell." There was no such thing as wall paint in Cuba in 1968. Shortly after, she moved in with her two children: a girl my sister's age and a boy two years younger than me. I never got along with her son. I really disliked him for some reason. My sister became friends with her daughter. Her daughter and I got along fine.

Shortly after they moved into our house and took over completely, I remember standing outside my room while a strange ritual took place inside my house. A beheaded chicken was being tossed and dragged throughout the house. The chicken's blood was being spilled all over the floor. I blocked out this moment of terror for many years until I was old enough to bring it back and understand what the ritual was all about.

Strange things happened after they took over our home. My stepmother claimed to be a medium. Once, when my sister and I were giving her a hard time and resisting her demands to clean, my father called us into their bedroom. It had been our bedroom, but now it was furnished with my mother's bedroom set, including my mother's mattress. She proceeded to pretend that the spirit of my mother was taking possession of her body. She called me *"mi hijita"* (my little daughter). I realized that she was a fake because my mother used to call me *"mi remanso"* (my peaceful refuge).

My poor mother! Oh my mother! How could someone just take her life and her things and her memory and disrespect her so much? I've never been able to get over that. Why didn't anyone stop her? I did not accept her behavior. I walked out of the room with an aching heart.

I became her servant, her messenger, and her experiment. She used to say that she had studied to be a nurse. My father trusted her enough that he would allow her to make medical diagnoses with regard to our health. She started to give me injections imported from Russia that she apparently obtained through the "black market" to help me grow because, according to the doctors that I do not recall having ever been to, I wasn't developing like all the other girls my age. Now I thank God for being healthy because I never found out what kind of injections they were. Many times I fainted right after she gave me the injections. I've never been so close to being lost forever as I was during that time.

Finally, the good news that we had been waiting for since before my mother's death arrived. I opened the front door one morning to find a man with a telegram. The man would make our trip to the United States possible. We were anti-revolutionaries and, although we had our visas, we still needed the permit that he was delivering to be able to leave Cuba on an airplane. I was standing next to my father when the man recited my mother's name, along with my father's, my sister's, and mine. I still remember my disappointment when I heard my father say that he was declining this opportunity since he had already applied to have his new family leave with us.

We had been waiting for this telegram to arrive for five

years prior to my mother's death. He never arrived and she died. Now he was there and we had a chance to join my mother's sister in the United States. My father was taking away our chance to be free again—out of Cuba. I felt angry, frustrated, and hopeless. I was tired of being sad and hungry—food was very scarce. My life became even harder after that day.

CHAPTER V
Liberation

FREEDOM IS probably the most important word in the dictionary. Yet everyone seems to take it for granted, including me who had to go through so much anguish and pain to experience its unmatched meaning. Nothing should be as important with the exception of health.

My family gave up everything in its search for freedom. We had enjoyed freedom before Fidel Castro's lies changed everything in Cuba. Not only did we have to give up our houses, but also my father had to give up his job, his status, his money, and all his possessions. He was then sent to work as a farmer.

During this time in Cuba, Fidel Castro implemented a cost-effective plan that could best be described as "farming expeditions" that would help expedite acquiring guns and bombs from Russia to defend Cuba from a possible attack by the United States. He would export goods to Russia, as he had done in the past, in exchange for weapons. However, this time he would force kids to work for free. The program consisted of groups of students who were only twelve- to eighteen-years old.

They would put them on buses (girls separate from boys) and ship them out to work as farmers for two months (less if you were a communist).

My sister and I were sent to work as farmers for two months. I don't recall my stepsister going with us. I never understood why or how she managed to get out of something that was totally mandatory for families who wanted to leave Cuba because they did not agree with the form of government.

If you were pro-revolution or communist, it was sort of an "elective" course that would reward you with extra credits in the form of goods and services. I'm not entirely sure how it worked. However, for those families that were against the revolution, it became mandatory—especially if you were one of those people who had been desperately waiting for years for the "man on a motorcycle" to stop at your house with a telegram. The telegram would contain a possible departure date when you would finally be able to leave Cuba.

If a parent who was against their form of government refused to send a child to work as a farmer, they would simply be denied the freedom to leave the country. During that time, this was the only legal way out for those who had applied to be able to leave Cuba.

Some people ended up waiting for years to hear back after applying and being exposed. Anyone who was exposed became known as a *gusano* (worm). Their lives became miserable and they had to surrender all of their possessions in return for the opportunity to leave Cuba, including homes, assets, clothing, and children's toys.

The government took an inventory of everything an applicant owned and expected everything to remain intact until they decided whether to allow the person to leave. Ultimately, people were only allowed to leave with clothing in one regular-sized suitcase. Children under the age of twelve were allowed to take one toy in addition to the suitcase.

We fell within that category. We had no choice but to comply with all of the requirements. We did not want to jeopardize our opportunity to finally leave Cuba. We had been waiting for eight years.

To make matters worse, we were very hungry because there was hardly any food. There was no orange juice or any other kind of juice—even though oranges and other fruits grow just about everywhere in Cuba. The shelves at the *bodegas*, and even the bakeries, were completely empty. There were no shoes or clothes to buy at the stores—not even underwear. There were no sanitary napkins.

A ration book was required to go to the store. Sometimes we would wait in line for hours only to find out that we were not entitled to whatever it is that we had been waiting for, whether it was potatoes, meat, chicken, eggs, or coffee. The reason for that was that, according to the ration book, we had already received those items. We realized that the items that we had been waiting for were only for those who had not gotten any the first time.

Guines was located about two or three hours from my home in Habana. It was one of the coldest areas in Cuba. The temperature felt like thirty degrees during November and December—and even colder without proper clothing.

My sister and I were sent to Guines in separate groups. They kept us separate the entire time. There were stables with two rows of bunk beds. The bunk beds were made of wood and had no mattresses; instead, the mattress section was made out of a very thin layer of some sort of rustic, non-insulated fabric. The windows of the stables were made out of concrete. Of course, there were no screens on these permanently open windows.

On a typical day, they woke us up at 5:30 with a whistle—as if we were prisoners. They forced us to exercise for approximately ten minutes before ordering us to get dressed without any privacy. Once dressed, they expected us to line up outside in the cold while waiting to use the latrine. Lastly, they would hand out watery hot chocolate with a slice of old bread as we walked toward the trucks that were parked waiting for us. By 6:00, we were being transported to the fields. Once there, we were expected to work for free for several very long hours.

The job consisted of picking potatoes, *malangas* (similar to potatoes), lettuces, and sweet potatoes. Sometimes we were expected to plant onions in the muddy terrain. I still remember how much I hated having to walk around full of mud after planting onions, mainly because I only owned one pair of work boots.

I recall the wooden boxes that said "For Export." We were not allowed to take any of what we picked and packaged to give to our families—and they watched us very closely to make sure that everyone complied. My father was a diabetic, yet I could not provide him with the *malangas* that I had heard were good for people suffering from diabetes. This was really upsetting to me.

One very cold morning, after having worked in the fields boxing *malangas* for export, I spotted some girls hiding some *malangas* under their shirts. At that moment, I started thinking about the many hours I had spent waiting in line back home for *malangas* or potatoes to be delivered to the market. Sometimes, even after waiting for hours, I still could not get my hands on any. Yet, here I was in the middle of a field packaging *malangas* to be exported to Russia.

I was worried that my father wasn't eating properly for his diabetes. I grabbed three or four *malangas* off the ground and stuck them inside my waistband. I was very petite, probably about seventy-five pounds, so I could not carry any more without being noticed.

Until that day, I had never stolen anything in my entire life—and I have never stolen anything else ever again. However, I justified my actions by thinking that I was not stealing since I was picking the *malangas* off the ground and not from the boxes. It almost felt right to take what was supposed to be mine in the first place. I recall that I only did it this one day because I was hoping that my father would come to visit me that coming Sunday.

I succeeded in transporting the *malangas* to the safety of a little wooden trunk where I kept my few belongings. I checked from time to time to make sure they were safe.

Somehow the women in charge found out that some of the girls had been stealing *malangas* from the fields. I heard a whistle and, shortly after that, a group of women came in shouting that there would be a search. We had to stand by our bunk beds and they started the search at the other end of the building. After listening to the other girls crying after the women confiscated their stolen goods, I panicked.

I ran as fast as I could while carrying my *malangas*. I felt embarrassed. Someone tried to grab me from behind as I was proceeding to exit the building. Strangely, I truly don't remember what happened after that.

Two or three weeks went by and things seemed to be getting progressively worse. I was very sad most of the time. I was only thirteen. After being raised in the city, it felt as if I was being punished for a crime I hadn't committed. I was being forced to function in such a bad environment. I wasn't just hungry, but also very cold. I only owned two pairs of jeans, two shirts, one worn-out sweater, and one pair of muddy work boots.

Upon returning from the fields every day, we would take a cold shower. We could only use warm water if we proved that we were menstruating. I would have to wash the muddy clothes by hand and hang them on a clothesline and hope for no rain. When it rained, sometimes I would have to wear the same muddy and smelly clothes from the previous day.

After working in the fields all morning, we would prepare for a late lunch in an open stable that they used as a lunchroom. I distinctively remember walking around the side of the stable after having worked hard one morning. I was extremely hungry.

A lady was cooking what looked like a pea soup in a big pot with a big wooden spoon. She was preparing to feed the entire crew. I was curious and looked to see how she was cooking. I saw what appeared to be chunks of Spanish sausage or some sort of meat with a few potatoes. I thought to myself how nice it would be if I could get a piece of meat in my bowl for a change. I sat down in my assigned spot and waited patiently for my soup.

They handed me my bowl and I got all excited because I was one of the lucky ones that had ended up with a piece of meat. I picked up the meat, but before I put it in my mouth, it moved. I quickly pushed it away from my face and realized that it was a grasshopper. Someone said that it had probably gotten into the soup while they were cooking it outside. I didn't care about what they said. I picked up the bowl and threw it across the room.

I came down with a fever the next day. I do not remember anyone giving me medicine to make the fever go down. I was so cold in my worn-out sweater and a thin, non-insulated blanket in bed that night. I was shaking uncontrollably from the cold and the fever. The bunk bed was shaking so badly that the girl sleeping underneath me decided to take a risk. Some prisoners from a nearby jail had escaped and we had been instructed not to go outside to the latrines, but she got my sister from a stable not far from ours. We were not supposed to hang around with the older girls and would get in trouble if we did.

My sister came over secretly through the back door and they both leaned over me with their blankets in an attempt to give me body heat until I stopped shaking. They took their blankets back because they were very cold. My sister managed to leave unnoticed. For the rest of the night, I was so cold that I thought I wasn't going to make it. No winter in the United States has ever made me feel as cold as I was that night in Cuba—not even during the five years I lived in Chicago.

It was devastating to realize that all of this was so that we could export goods to Russia in exchange for weapons—while there was nothing to eat in Cuba.

It is clear to me now that we were very much afraid of just about everything. Looking back now, I realize that spreading fear and intimidating tactics is most of what communism is all about.

We never found out whether there really was a jail nearby. I believe it was a tactic to keep us from escaping. No one would go outside because they kept telling us that there could be a rapist out there. They intimidated us to the point that you actually felt like you were doing something wrong if you got sick, and that it could get you in trouble.

They played with our minds. They kept us hungry and cold because then our lives became a struggle just to survive each day and there was no time left to think about anything else. They forced us to learn how to live without the basic necessities so that they did not have to provide them. The sad thing is that this went on across Cuba. Everything was being exported to Russia during that time.

Our entire family, including my two grandmothers, had already left Cuba when all of these things happened. They thought when they left that we were going to be able to leave Cuba a few days later. However, it did not work out that way.

My father was our only blood relative left in Cuba, but he had been sent to a farm. He could not come to visit because he had no transportation—even though he owned a car. He was missing one tire. There were no tires available for sale in Cuba in 1969.

Our neighbor who was a doctor had gotten a flat on his way to catch a clandestine chartered boat one night. He had asked my father if he could borrow his tire. That was the last night that we saw our neighbor. Ultimately, this trip reunited him with his wife and two children who had already left Cuba. They had been waiting for him in the United States. The Castro regime would not allow doctors to leave any other way. Of course, my father never got his tire back because our neighbor abandoned his car.

I could not wait to go home. I hated being at the farm. I was very hungry and cold most of the time. Every night I thought, *What happened to my life? What happened to my clothes, my dolls, my friends?* Thankfully, after completing the two-month mandatory stay at the farm, we were sent home. Afterward, we went back to school as usual.

A year later, I heard someone at the door during my mid-morning school break. I opened the door and the telegram man had returned. This time he had all the names right. He proceeded to take an inventory of every item in the house and compared it to the one on record from eight years earlier (when we first applied for permission to leave Cuba). Miraculously, everything was still there. He proceeded to put tape on our door while we watched, smiling, with very small suitcases in our hands with very little clothing.

Unfortunately, two days later, we had to break the seal and re-enter our home, because my father's attempts to legally adopt his stepson (his wife's son from a prior relationship) had not been finalized. We were back in our house after breaking the seal on the door, but our stinking house did not even feel like my house anymore

Unluckily, things really went downhill after that day—not only because we were not allowed back in school anymore, but because someone tried to kill one of us with a knife one beautiful evening while my sister, stepsister and I were sitting in our front porch.

Someone threw a knife across the front porch that barely missed us. My sister managed to lift her arm as the knife went under it. For some reason, I always suspected that my stepmother had something to do with it. She did not like my sister very much. She was nowhere to be found when it all took place and I went looking for her. She blamed our neighbor though. We never found out who did it. I don't recall the police ever showing up.

This incident brought back memories of when my mother

was being terrorized by a stranger while my father was working as a musician until early hours of the morning. On several occasions, she was sleeping in her room and a strange figure would show up outside her window. The stranger would light a match to look inside. However, the light from the match distorted the person's face and prevented her from being able to identify the intruder.

My father came home early a few times to try to catch who he assumed to be a man. However, the intruder was very quick and would simply vanish. One night I was sleeping in my mother's room when the stranger came to the window, lit a match, and proceeded to terrorize us for about ten minutes. However, he never came back after my mother passed away. Just as with the previous knife incident, they never caught the intruder. I have always wondered whether there was a connection between the two incidents.

A few months after this knife incident, the telegram man decided to come back a third time. This time, we were able to miraculously board an airplane headed for the United States of America. Just before we left Cuba, we visited the most beautiful beach in the world, Varadero. I've always been glad that we got to see that beautiful place before we boarded the airplane.

Although we liked being in Varadero, if only for a short time, we did not appreciate having to sleep in the abandoned house where they made us stay. This particular house, just like many others in Varadero, had been taken over by the communist government because of their close proximity to the airport. However, it was dirty and full of insects. Most of them used to belong to families that had already left Cuba. Still, that did not even matter. In the end, what really mattered was that we were finally almost free.

My father used to say that the first thing he would do upon getting off the airplane in the United States would be to kneel and kiss the soil. Although I did not witness him actually carrying out his plans, I am sure that he did.

CHAPTER VI
Closure

THIRTY YEARS after my mother's death, my father had his leg amputated due to complications from diabetes. I was with him at the hospital in Miami. It had taken him a long time to be able to talk to me about my mother. By then, he had been divorced from his second wife, blind, and to make matters worse, going through a most horrific experience.

Probably one of the best decisions I've ever made was to fly down to see him the night before the surgery. He seemed very sad and scared when I first saw him in the hospital room. I had asked the nurse not to let him know that I was there because I wanted to evaluate his condition on my own. I was watching him from a distance. I had never realized how courageous my father was. He had been blind for fifteen years and his health was deteriorating after such a hard life, but he still found a reason to live. He inspired me that night. His face lit up when he heard my voice. I stayed for a while and then kissed him good night. I came back the next morning to be there before they took him into surgery.

It wasn't until I was in my late thirties that I realized how hard my father's life really had been—and still was. His father died when he was only five years old. Then, Fidel Castro took over Cuba and took away everything he had ever worked for. Ultimately, he lost my mother. They had known each other since they were twelve years old and he adored her.

I still remember how he had burned all of her belongings immediately after her death. He built a fire next to our house and burned everything, including all of her pictures. As a kid—and even as a young adult—I never understood why we weren't even allowed to talk about her or even keep a picture of her. I realized much later in life that he was probably just mad at her for leaving him. Her death came so unexpectedly. It took my father thirty years to talk to me about my mother.

In the hospital room after his surgery, he told me that my mother had been the love of his life. We spent the ten days after his surgery just talking about the past, mainly to keep his mind off the present at least a while longer. I am glad that we talked because it brought us much closer.

He told me how my mother had died from a heart attack a few days after having surgery. I was kind of surprised because my mother had only been thirty-eight years old when she died and there was no history of heart disease in her family. We had always assumed that she had died from cancer.

I proceeded to tell my father how my grandmother Maria (who was the only person in the room with my mother when she died) had always told us that my mother's last words were, "I am having a reaction." Since it happened immediately after getting an injection from a nurse or aide at the hospital, she had assumed that it had been for pain. Apparently, my father had just stepped out of the room when my mother died. My father dismissed my comments. However, ever since our conversation, I have often wondered what really went on at that hospital. Unfortunately, we will never know what really happened.

My father was always thankful to God for allowing him to come to the United States. Like most Cubans who came to the United States in the late 1960s and early 1970s, he had hopes and dreams. He believed with all his heart that he was going to succeed financially again.

In Cuba, my father had been an accountant and real estate broker during the day and a musician at night. I still remember going to his office during the day and visiting him at the *Hotel Nacional* many times at night. He played two different kinds of saxophone in a very popular orchestra. After my father and mother got married, my father became very successful in real estate. The Shell Corporation had just acquired some land and he had been involved in the process. He managed to build three houses from scratch—our home and two other houses that he had rented out—and they provided us with extra income.

It all came crashing down one day when Castro confiscated all his savings and properties. Although he was only in his mid-thirties, this horrible disappointment affected his health. It was around that time that he became a diabetic.

Although he managed to pass the required real estate tests and had his accounting degree recognized in the Unites States, he never did get to succeed in those fields because of his health issues. He was never able to make it as a musician either. He eventually became blind from diabetes.

There are many reasons why I resented my father as I was growing up, but there is one decision he made that made up for everything I ever resented him for. His decision to leave Cuba and bring his family to the United States ultimately saved my life and made me learn to appreciate the meaning of freedom.

As the years went by, I even forgave him for declining our opportunity to leave Cuba in 1968, which was the first time the man came with the telegram. Although the telegram contained a possible departure date for us to leave, his declining the opportunity caused us to have to wait another year. We also ran the risk of having to stay in Cuba forever.

Chapter VII
The Miracle

WE ARRIVED in Miami, Florida, September 10, 1970. My Aunt Ofelia, my mother's sister, had been waiting for my sister and me. She had been waiting to start a family until our arrival.

My courageous Aunt Ofelia, along with her husband, was the first in my family to leave Cuba. In 1962, they realized that the Castro regime was not in the best interests of the Cuban people and that Cuba seemed to be headed for disaster.

My aunt and uncle had what they referred to as visa waivers or visas without restrictions, which allowed them to travel to the United States, just as my mother and father and many others in Cuba did. However, once Castro took over, no one was allowed to leave unless the government authorized it. In addition, someone in the United States needed to buy the tickets and claim financial responsibility for the family once they arrived in the United States.

My uncle, who had been working as a copywriter for a private publishing company when Castro took over, had recently been transferred to work within the department of communications of a major radio station in Habana known to promote the revolution worldwide. The fact that my uncle was bilingual and had no accent when he spoke English was an asset that they soon recognized and immediately started to take advantage of.

Although my uncle did not agree with the communist regime, he had no other choice than to pretend and act like a revolutionary in order to survive. However, my aunt and uncle realized that sooner or later he would be found out and that they needed to leave Cuba.

Since my uncle was considered a revolutionary, he was allowed to go on vacation to Moscow. During that time, my uncle and aunt had only been married for a couple of years and did not have any children. Accordingly, it would appear to be perfectly normal for them to plan a vacation.

In April 1962, they boarded a plane headed for Moscow. They were aware that the plane was scheduled to stop for fuel in Halifax. When they first boarded the plane, they were both sure that they would not be returning to Cuba. However, they had no definite plans as to how they would go about accomplishing this most dangerous operation.

While the airplane was fueling in Halifax, as they were stretching their legs on the runway, my aunt announced that she needed to run to the bathroom inside the terminal. She did not ask if she could go inside the terminal since she already looked a little suspicious with her carry-on luggage. She simply started running toward the terminal without looking back and motioning that she needed to go to the bathroom really badly. My uncle just followed.

Immediately after entering the terminal, my aunt spotted

an older man in uniform. He was wearing commemorative medals on his uniform, which gave the impression that he was someone important. She immediately ran over to him. She simply said, "I want to request political asylum." The man, who turned out to be a security guard, immediately replied, "Are you sure? Please repeat." My aunt said, "We want to request political asylum."

The plane was still waiting in the runway with approximately seventy-five revolutionary commanders. Some of them had already exited the airplane and were headed for the terminal. My aunt and uncle knew that they would be killed if they had to return to the airplane after asking for political asylum.

The security guard was fast to grasp the gravity of the situation. He immediately escorted them into a separate room inside the terminal and locked the door. He contacted the Secret Service who escorted them to the Department of Immigration while the plane continued to wait for them on the runway for approximately four hours. My aunt and uncle would always be grateful to the security guard who helped them at the airport and ultimately saved their lives.

They remained in an immigration jail in Halifax for two months until they were cleared by immigration. My aunt even fixed up the cell to look like a studio apartment. She decorated the little room with fresh flowers that she would pick every time she was allowed to go outside for a walk. Eventually, after my uncle was interrogated numerous times, they were cleared by immigration. Afterward, they were able to rent a room in someone's house. They lived in Halifax for about a year.

Then, one incredibly lucky day, my aunt's persistence paid off when she finally found a job in the United States with a leading bank in Washington. Once she cemented the job, the owner of a major beer manufacturer, whom she had met while working at the Board of Trade in Halifax, facilitated their trip to the United States. Eventually, they moved to Washington where they lived for approximately four years before deciding to move to Florida.

By the time we arrived in Florida in 1970, my aunt and uncle were already established financially in the United States. They had managed to buy a modest home, even after spending thousands of dollars helping most of our family members get out of Cuba, including my father and mother.

Initially, my aunt facilitated the tickets and required affidavits for her youngest sister and her family. They were able to leave Cuba in 1964 after attaining the necessary authorization from the Cuban government. During this time, my mother was still undecided and she did not take advantage of the fact that my aunt had gotten tickets for us to leave as well. However, by the time she made up her mind, Castro was not allowing anyone to leave. Later, my aunt's attempts to help my family get out failed, including a chartered vessel that was unable to get close enough to pick us up. Sadly, my mother passed away shortly after that.

My aunt also succeeded in helping my grandmother and uncle get out of Cuba by having them go to Spain first. They would end up living in Spain for six months while my aunt had to support them financially the entire time. They eventually made it to the United States. Later, my aunt also made it possible for my younger uncle and grandfather to get out as well. We miraculously made it to the United States in 1970.

When we finally arrived in Florida on September 10, 1970, my aunt made her intentions known to my father regarding having my sister and I move in with her. My aunt was still trying to get over my mother's death. They had been very close. The fact that she never got to see her sister before she died still bothers my aunt today. My aunt felt that it was her responsibility to help raise us. However, my father declined her offer and refused to let us stay with my aunt.

I was very disappointed, but excited about the future. I was amazed by all the things that I was experiencing, including the grocery store where I almost fainted the first time I entered it from the shock.

In Cuba, the shelves at the stores were completely empty. We had to use a ration book after waiting in line for hours. When something was delivered to the market, it usually did not last long enough to be put on the shelves.

I recall feeling dizzy as I entered the grocery store with my uncle a few hours after we arrived from Cuba. The lights seemed too bright. For a moment, I really thought I was dreaming. I had never seen so many items stocked up on shelves. It did not seem real to me.

I could not comprehend how there could be so many things to eat at this place, while there was nothing to eat in Cuba. Most amazing was my reaction when my uncle introduced me to the cheese spread—specifically the small can with the nozzle that makes the cheese come out. I remember rushing to his house to figure out how it really worked. Of course, the many varieties of crackers also contributed to my amazement.

Those memories are still very vivid in my mind. It felt as though I had gone from living in black and white to full color in just a few hours. I was totally amazed by the colors and the lights everywhere. I could not believe that there could be so many cars on one street. I remember reading every sign I came across—even though I did not understand most of them.

This was definitely one of the most fascinating and exciting experiences of my life.

To my surprise, the United States government made it possible for us to fly to New York two days later. They even provided us with coats prior to boarding the plane. We were now headed for New York—only two days after we had arrived in Miami.

We were considered political aliens. We were very lucky; it seemed as though we were actually welcomed into the United States with open arms. I was so happy to be free that it did not matter where they were sending me next. There are no words to describe how glad and fortunate I felt to have arrived in this wonderful place. Although my father had described the meaning of abundance many times, experiencing it was much more wonderful than I had anticipated it would be. I recall feeling grateful to the United States of America and to God for helping my family start a new life.

However, arriving in New York wasn't as pleasant as I had anticipated. The gray sky had an immediate negative impact on me. I missed Cuba's sunny sky. It was getting cold and I felt lonely and scared. My father's cousin was waiting for my father to arrive. She lived with her husband and daughter in a very dangerous area of New York. People used to get mugged while walking down the streets. I could hear the screams sometimes from the bedroom of our apartment.

My father's cousin found an apartment for us in a building across from hers. This turned out to be a very old third-floor, one-bedroom, and one-bath apartment with no elevator. The previous tenants had used one of the closets as a bathroom. We were a family of six. Besides the smell that took weeks to dispel—even though we spent hours cleaning—there was barely enough room to walk when we were all home at the same time.

This was a very hard time for me—a period of adjustment. I was now being forced to learn a new language in a school that appeared to be full of rich and snobby girls. I ended up going there because, according to my father's cousin, I would have never survived in the public schools where crime was very high.

At this private Catholic school in New York, the nuns used to put me in an empty classroom every day for approximately two hours with a Dictaphone. I was forced to listen to tapes to learn English. The rest of the time I became their experiment. I used to sit in the classroom listening to the instructions that I did not understand. The other girls made fun of my accent when I did manage to speak a few words. Yet, I was very lucky to be there since it was hard to get into that school.

My father's cousin had facilitated my admittance into this all-girls school. Although I was the same age as her daughter and in the same classroom as she was, she always undermined my efforts. She made me feel unwanted. She was not a very good student, but she was very popular. However, she really never helped me. I had no friends at that school except for a Cuban girl named Alicia. She was very sweet, smart, and nice.

Amazingly, although it took me several months before I started to understand English, I was able to get an A on my spelling tests. The nuns started to notice and made a big deal of it, which of course started to build my confidence. Once I was getting recognition, I wasn't viewed as dumb anymore. By the time I graduated from that school, I had already learned how to speak and write English. I even wrote a poem about love.

Amazingly, I won an award and a medal for becoming one of the best spellers in my class. Still, it was hard for me to carry on a conversation in English. Sadly, no one from my family was there to see me get my award. I was disappointed, but tried to convince myself that my mother was watching me from above. As always, I felt her presence.

Shortly after graduation, I was put on a plane with my newly born half-sister and shipped back to Miami where my father and his wife had been living for about a month. They had left my sister, my stepsister, and me with my grandmother and a fourteen-month-old baby. They were waiting for me to finish school while they were trying to find jobs in Miami. My father was very secretive so I had no idea until the day I was put on a plane with a baby that my life was changing again. I was only fifteen.

My sister, who was already engaged to be married, somehow managed to convince my father to let her stay with my grandmother in New York. While I was happy to move out of that horrible neighborhood in New York, I wasn't really prepared for the changes ahead.

My Aunt Ofelia was waiting at the airport after she found out that I was flying alone with the baby. She pleaded with my father to allow me to move in with her. She reminded him that I was only fifteen. She explained to him that it would be in my best interest to get a good education—and that she could facilitate that. She tried to make him realize that using me as a babysitter was not fair to me. She failed to convince him once again. However, somehow, after that argument at the airport, she managed to make him agree to allow me to spend every other weekend at her house.

I was totally confused and anxious not knowing what my

father's plans for my future really were. Going to my aunt's house every other weekend gave me hope.

I would end up living in Miami for three years—at the mercy of my father's new family. However, I still remember my uncle and aunt, along with their little daughter, faithfully coming to pick me up every other weekend. My grandmother lived with my aunt. Therefore, I really looked forward to finally being able to spend some time with my mother's family. Thankfully, this arrangement continued until the day I got married.

Needless to say, I have always been very grateful to my aunt and uncle for going out on a limb for me.

CHAPTER VIII
The Alternative

MOVING TO Miami initially appeared to be the end of my troubles. I enjoyed the weather very much. I also enrolled in high school and made new friends. I never suspected that one friend in particular would become like a sister to me.

Shortly after moving to Florida, I met a boy who was about my age. He was the son of my father's best friend. However, when my father found out that we had started seeing each other, he immediately discouraged us. Although he was a respectful and decent young man who would turn out to be a successful family man years later, he specifically told this young man to never attempt to see me again. I was upset. However, peace was the best alternative and I somehow found a way to come to terms with his decision.

Shortly after breaking up with my boyfriend (who only held and kissed my hand as we danced the one time we were alone), I met up with my neighbors from Cuba. They were known in my former neighborhood as "the twins." The twins' sister was my sister's best friend.

One of the twins, Leonardo, made it clear from the beginning that he liked me. I was sixteen at the time and he was twenty-one. He had a steady girlfriend when I met him. However, a few weeks later, he broke up with her. Shortly thereafter, we started seeing each other exclusively. I liked the fact that he appeared very masculine and mysterious. I thought that I had found love—or maybe I wanted it to be love.

It was hard being home with my father's new family. I was exhausted most of the time. I worked part time after school every day. I used to get home around seven most nights. I still was expected to take care of my little sister. It was clear that I needed some distraction. Dating Leonardo seemed to be the most rational solution to me. I assumed that my father would not object to our relationship because he was older and he had known his family for many years.

Although my father objected at the beginning, he allowed us to start seeing each other as long as there was a chaperone with us at all times. Every time Leonardo came to visit, a member of our family would have to sit in the living room with us while we watched television.

The same rules applied whenever we went anywhere. We were never allowed to be alone—other than the brief good-byes right outside the door where we managed to kiss briefly. That was simply the way it was. Those were the Cuban traditions and my father made me abide by them—regardless of how I felt. As time passed, my father became even stricter. He gave us no flexibility.

In addition, I was expected to give my stepmother ten of my hard-earned thirty dollars from my paycheck. She would turn around and use that to buy herself clothing and jewelry—the same items that I could not afford to buy for myself after having to pay for my own lunch and transportation expenses.

I had to buy myself whatever clothing I needed to survive. I only owned two or three outfits—and hopefully enough underwear to last me the entire week. Thank God that they provided the laundry detergent so that at least I was able to do my laundry. In my world, there was no such thing as going shopping at the mall. It was all work and no play.

It was clear from the beginning that my father and his new family never looked out for my best interest. They never encouraged me to go to college. On the contrary, they made it clear that I was supposed to go out and find a full-time job after my high school graduation.

During a big argument with my father and his wife, wherein they tried to break us up, Leonardo told my father that he would continue to see me no matter what. Shortly thereafter, we got engaged. Six months later, we started planning our wedding.

We got married in October 1974—a month after graduating from high school. Although my stepmother managed to convince my father that I was not, I was a beautiful, young, inexperienced, eighteen-year-old virgin when I got married.

We managed to have a really nice wedding at a country club, which we ended up having to pay for later. My father and his wife gave me a blanket as their wedding present after learning that we were moving to Chicago. Our plans were to drive to Chicago for our honeymoon. Supposedly, Leonardo had a job waiting for him there.

As it turned out, there was no job for Leonardo in Chicago. Consequently, we ended up having to live with his relatives for almost six months. Even though I was fortunate enough to find my first full-time job, my salary was not enough to cover our expenses.

While I was working in the personnel department, I had access to all the job openings and was able to help Leonardo find a job. Immediately after he found a job, we managed to get our first apartment at a cheap hotel that allowed us to pay weekly, which made it a little easier to afford.

Finally, a year after arriving in Chicago, things were starting to look promising and we prospered. We had our own apartment in a very nice development where we made friends and felt somewhat happy.

One day after going for my regular checkup, I was told by my gynecologist that I had a deviated pelvis. The doctor explained that I would most probably never be able to conceive a child. Although we were not planning to start a family, I remember mentioning the doctor's comments to Leonardo. Even though I was somewhat upset about the news, I thought that it was nice just being married with no kids—especially now that we were living very comfortably. We both had fairly reasonable salaries.

The news about being pregnant took me by total surprise. I could not understand how someone could get pregnant while using protection. It never occurred to me that my husband had lied to me. It appeared that we had been having unprotected sex for quite some time without my knowledge. That is what being young and naïve is all about. I felt that my life was changing again and that I had no control over it. On one hand, I was delighted to be carrying a child, but on the other hand, I was terrified.

Being pregnant was the easy part. However, having the baby was an entirely different story. I almost lost my life due to an oversight. While the doctors were getting ready to take me into surgery for a cesarean after sixteen hours of labor, my anesthesiologist was called to an emergency surgery. By the time my regular doctor got back to me, I was already in distress.

To make matters worse, a fairly new anesthesiologist who ultimately came to my rescue messed up by injecting the spinal anesthesia as I was having a contraction. This caused my lungs to collapse. I was not able to breathe and passed out. According to my daughter's father, it took a while for the doctors to bring me back.

Some believe that we are given a few opportunities throughout our lives to exit this world—should we choose to do so. I believe that this was probably my first because I died briefly during the surgery. I saw a bright light—sort of like a tunnel—the same way some books describe the brief previews of the afterlife. I was not able to breathe and someone's voice called out my blood pressure as it dropped.

I felt my mother's presence very near. At the same time, I remembered that I was having a child and that I could not leave it alone. I reasoned with whoever was there at that magical place with me. I communicated telepathically and implored to be allowed to stay to take care of my child. When I heard her cry, every ounce of energy kicked in. I miraculously managed to bring myself back from the other side. Surprisingly, there she was—the most beautiful and cutest little girl I had ever seen.

After the surgery, I was totally exhausted and unable to enjoy my sweet baby girl right away. Still, I considered myself very lucky to be alive. I would soon realize that I had to pick a name for her. For some strange reason, I had been expecting a boy. I ended up naming her after my mother.

I almost died that day. It took me almost two weeks to regain enough strength to go home with my daughter. Eventually, I did go home and became this little girl's mom.

Looking back, I still consider giving birth and becoming a mother the most beautiful, spiritual, and amazing experience of my entire life.

CHAPTER IX
The Painful Truth

BY 1979, we had been living in Chicago for approximately four years. One night, Leonardo said, "Let's move back to Florida." Our daughter was eighteen months old. We had been working different shifts at work in order to be able to care for our daughter, since the babysitters had turned out to be unreliable. Since we hardly got to spend time together, our marriage and sex life were affected.

I initially resisted the idea of moving to Florida, but then I started to imagine a new life in a sunny city. I was starting to feel very lonely in Chicago. Strangely, Leonardo sometimes would go out shopping and not return home for hours on the weekends. After returning home, he would tell me that he had gone window-shopping all those hours. Amazingly, I would believe his stories. He was very convincing. I was all alone with my daughter most of the time. I wanted very much to have my family around. However, I had forgotten that I really did not have any close family to begin with.

In 1980, we moved back to Florida after almost five years.

At first, I had to struggle to find a job that would pay at least close to what I had been making in Chicago. After I found the job, I started to feel stressed with a very active toddler.

A few months later, Leonardo was able to find a job in Florida. We decided that, since he was making enough money, I would stay home to take care of our daughter. Even though money was tight, I was happy to be home with my child. However, after a year, I had no choice but to go back to work.

I was working at a bank when Leonardo was arrested. He had been charged with sexual misconduct in a public bathroom. However, the charges were eventually dropped. Apparently, his lawyer was able to convince the judge that it had been a case of mistaken identity. Nevertheless, this particular incident left me feeling drained. Leonardo was very convincing. He kept insisting, with tears in his eyes, that he had been unjustly accused. Again, I wanted very much to believe him, so I eventually did.

Thankfully, it was during this time that I started working for a family-owned—and very prosperous—corporation. This particular relationship ended up having a positive impact on my life.

It appears that God sends certain people into our lives when we most need them. Not only did the owner become my employer, he also ended up changing the way I looked at life and became my mentor. One morning, while I was working in his company, I got a call from our doctor, letting me know that my husband was being admitted to the hospital.

That phone call was the beginning of a very painful chapter in my life. However, I am very grateful that this wonderful person took the time out of his busy schedule to give me advice—just when I needed that kind of help the most. Sometimes listening to his encouraging speeches was enough to empower me. He took the time to explain that we are never alone. He taught me that a family can consist of just one person—as long as you manage to keep it together.

One morning, he called me into his office and handed me an airplane ticket to go see my sister in New York. Initially, I refused to accept it, but he insisted. He said that he had purchased the ticket for me because he wanted me to be able to look at life from midair. He wanted me to look out the window of the airplane and realize how big this world really is. He wanted me to understand that my life was not limited to my present circumstances.

Ultimately, he taught me that, even when we do fall, we can get up again and again—as long as we have our health and our eyes can see what's coming. I later learned that he had been diagnosed with a very rare disease that was slowly stripping him of his eyesight.

It was shortly after that trip that I moved back to New York. As we said good-bye, he said that his only request of me was an annual Christmas card. To date, I have sent him twenty-seven Christmas cards and have received twenty-seven cards back.

Yes, I had a good job and that job would eventually open the door to another good job, but only because of this man's kindness and good references.

CHAPTER X
The Betrayal

ONE DAY in 1982, I met a young man in the hospital elevator. It was evident that he had been crying. He was tall, very slim, and had dark hair and brown eyes. He was not particularly attractive and seemed somewhat filthy. He was probably nineteen or twenty.

My husband had been admitted to intensive care because of his incredibly high blood pressure. His doctor feared that he could have a heart attack. As I rode the elevator, I couldn't help but notice that the young man was extremely upset. I asked him if he was there to see a family member.

He told me with tears in his eyes that he was there to see a friend who had just been admitted to intensive care. I thought that there would be more than one person in intensive care that day. As it turned out, he was there to see my husband.

I don't remember why or how it was arranged for me to meet with my husband's doctor when he came out of the hospital. As I waited nervously for my appointment, I could not understand why my husband was not there with me to see his doctor. It turned out to be a very strange consultation.

"You need to sit down with your husband. There is something that he needs to tell you," said the doctor.

"I don't understand. Why don't you just tell me what it is?" I asked.

"It is something very delicate that you need to hear from him, but that I feel would definitely improve his health," the doctor replied.

I went home with many different scenarios repeating in my head. I was so worried about my husband. I really cared about him and wanted whatever it was to get resolved. I rushed home determined to get to the bottom of the problem.

I was in bed with my husband at around one o'clock on that March morning. He was the most important person in the world to me at that time. I had known him since I was two. In a photograph from my fifth birthday, he was pulling the string of my *piñata*.

I said, "I believe that there is something that you need to tell me."

There was no answer, but I persisted.

"What's wrong?" I asked.

"It was true, you know, the incident in the public bathroom," said Leonardo.

"What do you mean?".

"I just need to be by myself, I think," said Leonardo. "I am going to need some time to figure out what it is that I really want."

"What are you saying?"

"He has the same problem."

"Who are you talking about?" I asked.

"My brother," said Leonardo.

He explained how he and his twin brother were bisexual. He implied that he needed to explore his feelings to figure them out. He implied that he expected me to accept his behavior for as long as necessary. I immediately suspected the young man in the elevator. It felt as if someone had stabbed me in the heart.

I threw up in the bathroom with my head inside the toilet for a very long time. I was shocked, numb, and sick at the same time.

The first thing I thought of the next morning was to call my sister-in-law—not his sister, but my other sister-in-law—the other victim. I called the wife of his twin brother and invited her over for lunch. I had planned what I was going to say. I thought that if we both were going through it at the same time, it would be less painful, less shameful, and less confusing.

She was very happy and her face looked radiant as she walked into my condominium. She immediately announced that she also had something to tell me. I told her that I needed to talk to her as well. I asked her to tell me her news first.

She told me with a big smile on her face that she was pregnant with her second child. Tears filled my eyes and I had to look away to hide my disappointment. She asked me to tell her my news. I do not remember what I said to her, but whatever I ended up telling her was definitely not what I had originally planned to tell her—not after what I had just learned. I allowed her to leave with her heart still filled with the joy of expecting another child.

It wasn't until a week or so later that I announced the news to everyone. I did not have the heart to tell his family the truth about his brother. His brother continued to lie to his wife for four more years.

I remember the afternoon that I woke up in shock. A month or so had passed since that horrible night when I had asked him to tell me the truth—not realizing how painful it would turn out to be. He had already moved out of our apartment. I was in the process of selling everything and finding a place to live. I was trying to sell anything and everything that reminded me of him and what we once had.

I was at a Pizza Hut with my daughter after work—the same place we had gone many times as a family. I remember thinking how I would never, ever, allow myself to miss anyone as much again. I hated myself for having been so blind. I promised to never open my heart to anyone again.

Although we were divorced, Leonardo would continue to lie for many years. He claimed that he was the victim because I was making him pay by not allowing him to spend time with his daughter. He lied about not paying child support. He lied to his boyfriend for years, making him believe that I was draining him financially. He had stopped paying me child support shortly after our divorce.

Eventually, his hurtful behavior and lies—along with his lack of kindness and concern for his daughter by not worrying about her welfare—are what would end up hurting me more than the actual lie about who he really was during the eight years we were married. Still, I never really judged him. I simply walked away, but I was never the same. The love that I thought I felt for him died that night with my head stuck in that toilet.

You have to have been victimized in order to be able to define the meaning of betrayal. It is one of the most debilitating feelings because it strips you of your most powerful defenses such as confidence and self-esteem. It can leave you feeling helpless, lost, scared, and scarred for the rest of your life—but only if you let it.

The recovery is slow, but more powerful than anyone could possibly anticipate. You have to have faith in yourself and faith in God. You will become stronger and more human than you could have possibly imagined. You also become more receptive and perceptive. Slowly, your confidence returns and you somehow learn to trust again.

CHAPTER XI
The Solution

IN 1982, there was no such thing as the Internet—or any kind of support group for that matter. The experience of going through a divorce was traumatic enough without the added shame of my husband having been unfaithful to me with another man.

During that time, there were no other known cases to compare my situation to. The 2006 case involving the New Jersey governor's wife—except for the fact that her husband was a powerful man—was very similar to mine. Similar to Dina Matos McGreevy's daughter, my daughter was very young (five years old) when I ended up divorced and all alone. There is no way anyone can possibly know how it feels to go through something so traumatic—unless she actually goes through it.

My first priority became getting divorced. I retained legal counsel and started the divorce proceedings. I also enrolled in some college courses and started attending classes a couple of nights per week. One night after class, as I was walking through the college parking lot to get to my car, I noticed a man's figure in the distance watching me. I became very concerned. It wasn't long before I realized that my soon-to-be ex-husband was stalking me.

He continued to stalk me to the point where I had to stop attending college. Not only would he wait for me in the parking lot, but he would also follow me in his car wherever I went. This continued for months—even after our divorce was final.

Once the divorce was final, the woman in me cried out for help. I thought that I must have done something wrong to deserve such an outcome. Perhaps, as a woman, there was something that I was supposed to have done sexually that I did not do, which caused my husband to leave me for a man.

Looking back, I realize how illogical all of my thoughts were. However, at that time, going through it, they were the logical psychological responses of a healthy, beautiful, passionate twenty-five-year-old woman.

My second priority became finding a real man. This, to my surprise, turned out to be easier than I had anticipated. It happened one night while I was having dinner with friends at a restaurant. I found the most beautiful brown eyes staring at me. Our instant sexual connection made me feel a way I never had before. My inexperience in this field was evident, but I did not pick up on it at the time. All I wanted to do was to be with a man—and the man had just arrived.

Felix was tall and very attractive. It wasn't long before we started an intense sexual relationship that had begun with a kiss the night we met.

My ex-husband soon realized what was happening. Almost immediately after I met Felix, he waited for me to come home one day. He grabbed my hair as I was exiting his car after he asked me to sit inside to discuss the reasons why he did not have the child support money that week. He nearly killed me that afternoon.

This incident took place in my aunt's driveway. My daughter and I had temporarily moved into her guesthouse. Instead of discussing his failure to keep his promises, we ended up having an argument over Felix. During this argument, he informed me that I was to remain single for the rest of my life and devote my life to our daughter. Ultimately, my uncle had to come out with a gun to convince him to let go of my hair.

This incident only brought me closer to Felix. Soon we were more involved than I was ready for. I moved out of my aunt's guesthouse into my own one-bedroom apartment near my job. Felix would stay over at my place most weekends because his job was about an hour away and it only made sense for him to stay with my daughter and me. Soon, however, he started sleeping over sometimes during the week as well.

Sooner than later, my ex-husband picked up on the fact that Felix was sometimes staying over. He proceeded to contact my family and they began calling me to express their concern. At some point, I was told that my ex-husband had the right to take my daughter away because I was living with another man. I was young and ignorant.

Once again, I was thinking that I was doing something wrong. I did not realize that none of these people were worrying about me having enough to eat. They were more concerned about the family's reputation being tarnished by my actions. However, it never occurred to me that they were being influenced by my ex-husband who was once again spreading false rumors about what was really going on in my life.

He continued to stalk me and make my life miserable. He would call and lie to my family by telling them that I was acting inappropriately in front of his daughter. Even though he had already stopped paying child support, he managed to convince my family that I was taking advantage of him financially while I lived with another man.

He would come to my house and start a conversation with Felix just to plant doubts in his mind. Later on, I realized that he had made up stories about me having other relationships to make my boyfriend jealous.

He would lie to the police by calling and saying that the man living with me was abusing his daughter. The police would arrive unexpectedly—sometimes as we would be getting ready to sit down to have dinner—in response to his false complaints. However, soon the police picked up on the fact that my ex-husband was just creating trouble for me. They eventually picked up on the fact that I was a good mother and stopped coming over to check up on us.

His actions continued to make our lives a living hell. He would not pick up his daughter when he was supposed to. When he did pick her up, he would not drop her off when he was supposed to—just to make me nervous.

I had only known Felix for two months when he asked me to marry him. I was so vulnerable and susceptible during that time that I ended up marrying him.

CHAPTER XII

The Strange Man I Married

JEALOUSY WAS something new in my world, but it was most debilitating. As it turned out, Felix turned out to be so insecure that caused him to become extremely jealous—and even violent at times.

The ax took residence in my pantry, just hanging there staring at me. Felix put it there and would occasionally unhook it and show it to me from a distance so I would be aware of its presence.

While the sex was still great, at times it was excessive. It became sort of his way of wearing me down—to make sure that I had no energy left in me to even look at another man. I picked up on that little by little—just as I picked up on the fact that we were headed for disaster.

Felix grew progressively violent every time we had a fight and my marriage became a nightmare. He became obsessed with me. He would get mad if I came home from work five minutes late. He became so jealous that I could not even look out the window. I soon realized that I had to find a way to leave him. After one big fight, I decided to pack a suitcase and gather most of my daughter's toys. I eventually managed to leave him.

Late that night, my daughter was asleep in her room. He threw me on our bed and grabbed me by my neck. He wanted me to tell him how many men I had gone to bed with before him. I couldn't breathe. I kicked him hard, but he was much stronger. I was just about dead when I managed to tell him that I would haunt him for the rest of his life if he left my daughter without a mother. He let go of my neck and I was able to breathe again.

Suddenly, I realized what his ex-wife had been trying to communicate to me through her eyes every time we would go to pick up his daughter. Perhaps she was trying to warn me about his outbursts. His daughter was the same age as mine was.

I could never understand why he left his ex-wife. She seemed to be a very nice person and they had a beautiful daughter together. I suspected that was why he was always nice and very respectful toward my daughter. She probably reminded him of his own daughter. He also tried to control his temper whenever she was around. However, I started to realize that sooner or later that too could change.

My sister had been trying to convince me to move back to New York since my divorce from my daughter's father was finalized. I really could not afford to make the move. However, this time she realized how scared I was and she asked me to consider moving in with her and her family temporarily. She was living in Staten Island at the time. I had visited her several times and really liked the area.

The night after our fight, I pretended to fall asleep next to him. I had already planned my escape during prior incidents, but they had not been as scary as this one was. One time, he put his fist through the wall and only stopped short when he was about ready to punch me. Another time, he threw a fan across the room in a rage that almost hit me.

My sister was nice enough to fly down to help me escape, but I had already left my house with the help of friends by the time she arrived at the airport. I wanted to go back to retrieve some of my belongings before Felix got back from work, but my sister convinced me otherwise by making me realize how dangerous it was. I ended up leaving not only him, but everything I owned. I had my life and my precious daughter and that was all that mattered to me.

Leaving was painful and upsetting beyond words—especially after what I had gone through with my daughter's father only two years earlier. Somehow, it was an awakening that filled me with strength.

This experience forced me to learn how to survive on my own with my daughter. It is how I eventually learned the meaning of endurance, patience, and gratitude.

In retrospect, this experience was the only reason why I ended up moving to Staten Island. Without it, I would have never ended up moving back to New York—and five years later, New Jersey. It was in New Jersey that I ended up meeting my present husband, Tony. It is also where my daughter met her husband some years later.

CHAPTER XIII
A New Beginning

I FOUND a job the second day after moving to Staten Island. January 2, 1984, was one of the coldest days in New York City. I was very proud of myself after the man at the employment agency told me the news. I was planning to start my new job the following Monday, but I couldn't have done it without my good friend's references from my job in Florida—the gentleman to whom I promised I would send the Christmas cards.

Although my sister was nice enough to let us move in with her family, it wasn't long before I realized that it was time for me to go. My sister had two young children and her husband was the only one working. Although I contributed toward my own expenses and managed to pay them back for the plane tickets, I still felt that I had inconvenienced them enough. A month after I started working, I had saved enough to be able to move into my own apartment with my daughter.

After about six weeks, I was able to put a down payment on an efficiency apartment not too far from my sister's house. My sister was nice enough to continue watching my daughter after school until her public school implemented an after school program.

I realized that I was starting out with nothing for the third time in my life. I bought a sofa bed, a table, four chairs, and some kitchen utensils on credit. I eventually was able to pay to have my car shipped from Florida. That was the beginning of my new life.

I remember my eyelashes freezing while I waited for the bus to come at seven o'clock each morning to go to work. My commute was one and a half hours each way. I ended up working in New York City for five years.

Approximately a year after moving to Staten Island, I met Marc. I was twenty-eight and he was six years older. I don't remember what I found most irresistible: the way he softly kissed my hand when we met or his captivating brown eyes. Nonetheless, we started dating. Marc was originally from Florida. He had a calm, easygoing personality. I felt very happy whenever we were together. Although our relationship was mostly sexual, we still managed to develop a great friendship.

Unfortunately, Marc eventually ended up admitting that he was just "temporarily" separated from his wife, who still lived in Florida with his son. I found this out four months after we started dating. Shortly after that, we stopped seeing each other.

I felt hurt because Marc hadn't been truthful from the beginning. Nevertheless, he did help me regain my confidence and taught me much about sexuality and sensuality. Even though I swore that I wasn't going to date anyone ever again, I have always been glad that our paths crossed when they did. Although I have to admit that it did take me a while to get over Marc, I eventually found the strength to pull myself together.

A few weeks after Marc and I went our separate ways, I had the most uplifting experience. It was a week before Christmas 1984 and I had been working at my job for almost a year. However, I was struggling financially. Leonardo, as usual, was ignoring his financial responsibility toward his daughter. He had stopped paying child support. Some nights, I recall struggling to find anything to cook for dinner.

I was very sad that Christmas, mostly because I was struggling financially. To make matters worse, my daughter had asked for a special doll that year for Christmas that I could not afford. A Cabbage Patch Kid was the only toy on her list. I was upset, but I don't remember mentioning it to anyone.

I distinctively remember getting to work one very cold December morning after my long commute. As I took off my coat, I noticed an envelope on my desk. There was money and a letter inside the envelope. The letter was signed by "Santa."

Someone had taken the time to write the most thoughtful letter. It said that since Santa did not know what my daughter wanted for Christmas, he had decided to give me money so that I could buy her a gift. My eyes filled up with tears of joy. There turned out to be one hundred and seventy-five dollars in that envelope.

I never found out who wrote the letter or even whether it was from just one person or more. It did not matter to me. What really mattered was the fact that the letter brought back my faith in humanity. Amazingly, this turned out to be the most special Christmas of my life. I was able to watch my daughter, with great joy, play with her Cabbage Patch Kid.

Incredibly, two months later, I got a raise at work. Then, six months later, I was able to transfer to a better paying job within the same company. I immediately started to recover financially and eventually stopped struggling. I even had money left over that spring to take my daughter to an amusement park. It was clear to me that God was watching over my family. I continued to pray. I also managed to start meaningful friendships that have lasted for many years and created beautiful memories.

In the fall of 1985, I met Tony. It was hard for me to go out by myself because I could not afford a babysitter. However, my landlord was nice enough to offer to watch my daughter so that I could go out for a while. I went dancing to a nice nightclub in New Jersey with my girlfriend from work.

I was standing by the bar with my girlfriend when Tony came over and asked me to dance. Strangely, I immediately felt safe with him. He seemed older and very confident. Although I found him attractive, it was his energy that instantly energized my soul. Surprisingly, I found out he was also from Cuba. He had moved to the United States with his family in 1962. It was strange to find someone from Cuba, especially in the area where this nightclub was located.

When I told Tony that I was from Cuba, we became instant friends. He was divorced with two children. Shortly after we met, he told me about an experience he had years back involving a woman he dated for a very long time who turned out to be a lesbian. He then explained how much this experience had affected his life.

At first, I thought he was kidding—but he wasn't. I told him how my ex-husband had managed to live a double life during the eight years we were married. I explained how he had managed to conceal the fact that he was gay, just as his girlfriend had concealed the fact that she was a lesbian.

These coincidences made us realize that we were meant to be together. We became really good friends. I also became very good friends with his sister. We ended up living together for seven years before deciding to get married.

I am convinced that it was God that brought us together twenty-five years ago.

CHAPTER XIV
Our Gift from God

WHEN MY daughter was fifteen, I went through the hardest chapter in my life. It probably brought me the closest to God, but it left me totally powerless for some time.

In 1992, I was sitting in my girlfriend's car trying to make sense of what was happening. She reminded me that my daughter was very much alive. Her daughter had passed away suddenly only two years earlier. She was helping me to prioritize the events as they were taking place. She was trying to force me back into the present where I very much needed to be if I was going to face what was coming my way.

I went home and collapsed in bed just as I had every day since my daughter broke the news to me that she was pregnant. A few days earlier, my fifteen-year-old daughter had told me that she was pregnant. How could my beautiful daughter—my pride and joy—be doing this to me, to us? I felt as if someone had kidnapped her and an arrow had gone through my heart.

In the days after my daughter broke the news about her pregnancy, I fell into a deep depression. For days, I did not want to get out of bed. I just wanted to sleep all day. I had already missed two or three days of work. When Tony came to check up on me, he had never seen me so depressed. He was used to my active personality.

While this was taking place, Tony and I had been together for seven years. Although we had talked about getting married a few times, we had not yet set a date. In retrospect, we were very happy just living together. We loved each other very much. I felt that we had a good thing going. Subconsciously, we were probably afraid of ruining what we had by getting married.

On this particular painful day, Tony somehow managed to force me out of bed. He simply said, "Let's go to the store to buy a crib." I did not understand at first, but he insisted. I don't even remember getting dressed. All I remember is that we went and bought a crib. I do recall it being a very nice experience. Strangely, buying that crib allowed me to see the wider picture and helped me move forward. Almost immediately, I started to get over my depression.

What I have always loved most about Tony is his zest for life. His love and excitement about life have always helped me make it through the hard times. Tony has always been there for me—since the day we met—no matter what. Although we have had our ups and downs along the way, we still have managed to keep it going.

I will always be grateful to Tony for not giving up on me during the most difficult time in my life. Without him, I probably would not be as positive, confident, and optimistic as I am today. I believe that it is his love all these years that has helped me keep the faith and remain strong. Ultimately, his persistence ended up helping me to get over my depression.

We made an appointment with a doctor the next day. I was

considering trying to convince my daughter to have an abortion, but she was determined to have her baby. I was prepared to discuss this option with the doctor while we were in the waiting room. They called my beautiful daughter into the room for her sonogram. A little while later, they called me into the room—and that is when I met him. My beautiful grandson was looking right at me from the monitor. Suddenly, I realized that there was a force much stronger than any apparent reason behind it all. I immediately dismissed the idea of an abortion.

I distinctively remember bumping into one of the nurses as I was exiting the sonogram room. She looked at me and said, "It's a good thing that you are young and will get to watch your grandson grow up. Some people die before they get to meet their grandchildren." For a moment, I felt my mother's presence in that hallway—and then the nurse disappeared into one of the other rooms.

Nevertheless, the events made it hard to cope. A test came back abnormal and they had to do more testing to make sure that the baby was healthy. Fortunately, we had a very good doctor who kept us well informed. After almost a month of endless tests and waiting for the results, we were able to come to terms with the fact that a healthy baby boy was on his way to us. The good news made us very happy.

We contemplated the idea of having my daughter marry her boyfriend. We thought for a while that it would be the best solution. We initially planned to have him move in with us after the wedding. It turned out that the best decision we ever made was not to have a wedding. Both the young man and my daughter were too young to settle down. In time, we realized that they were still children.

I never got a chance to plan my daughter's Sweet Sixteen

party. Instead, her girlfriends from high school organized a surprise baby shower for her. Yet, for some unknown reason, it all felt very natural. Strangely, it became clear to me that this baby, this soul, was meant to become part of our family.

We had a choice and we chose "life," a beautiful "life." Yet society did not seem to be on our side, as many people judged us. Some even implied that I was irresponsible and careless for allowing my daughter to get pregnant. Although, in my heart, I knew that was not true, I did end up blaming myself.

On the other hand, during that critical time, my daughter needed understanding and moral support in order to remain healthy. We became determined to guide her the best way we knew how—despite all the censure. Ultimately, my daughter's courage while going through it all is what surprised us all the most in the end. She managed to continue attending high school despite all the criticism. But, most amazingly, she managed to deliver a beautiful, healthy baby.

Some people criticized us for taking over and adopting our grandson. However, no one stopped to realize that we needed to provide a stable environment for him as well as for my daughter. We had medical bills that needed to be paid, but no one offered any kind of financial assistance. I guess it was easier for some to judge than to help us out.

Eventually, I stopped listening to people since it was affecting us as a family. Their tactless comments were causing me to blame and judge my daughter—as well as myself. Eventually, I realized that we needed to focus if we were going to survive as a family. I needed my daughter to know that we loved her very much and that we were there for her—even though, at times, it seemed as if we were going against the world.

There was not much help back then. Even now, it seems as

if there is not enough help out there for grandparents like us. No one realizes that, in some instances, it is the grandparents who end up raising the children of their children. In most cases, the children are neither mature enough nor capable of taking on such a big responsibility.

Furthermore, most people fail to recognize that the young men often do not end up contributing to their child's welfare. Moreover, they fail to recognize that it is hard for children to take care of their own children simply because they are still children themselves.

We can go on forever about how unfair it all was then—and perhaps still is today. However, the fact remains that a child is no less a child because his or her mother is a teenager. The teenager is no less a person because she or he is having a child. The babies eventually become adults while society continues to condemn and censure, making the parents' and grandparents' jobs more difficult than they have to be.

Unfortunately, I suspect that nothing will actually change until society's relationship toward teenage pregnancies becomes more realistic. Ultimately, I believe that it is what it is because it is all part of a much bigger plan—God's plan. My grandchild is a precious gift.

I realize how lucky we were during that difficult time because we had the freedom and the resources that helped us make the informed choices that we had to make.

I recognize the need for better laws, more love, and less prejudice in our society, but I feel blessed and privileged for having been able to raise my children in the United States. The best thing about living in the United States is that you can always hope that things are going to get better. In retrospect, I realize that my most difficult times in the United States have been only setbacks—especially when compared to the dead years that I lived through in Cuba.

Finally, I recognize how lucky we are to wake up every morning with freedom and hope. This realization, at the end of each day, ends up renewing my soul.

Epilogue

IT SEEMS to be all about the experience. I believe there is something to be learned and remembered from every situation—even when it turns out differently than what we expected or wanted with all of our hearts.

While flying home from a vacation with my husband and dear friends, I decided to finish writing this book. Perhaps it was the thrill of ziplining through the Costa Rican jungle—soaring above the treetops—that ultimately inspired and energized me.

Although I remain uncertain about the future, I feel blessed, grateful, unafraid, and in a good state of mind. Strangely, I seem to have a new purpose these days.

Living in the present and not taking anything for granted in this life are the most important lessons I've learned. By living in the present, I get to see the wider picture.

I have learned that happiness comes from the smallest and simplest things and experiences. Still, at times, if we are not fully aware and perceptive, it tends to fade away before we have had a chance to recognize it. It also seems that happiness, just as a butterfly that is pursued, only comes to us when we wait quietly without expectation. It seems to be all about the little things, the precious moments, and the precious gifts.

I believe that there is still much that I need to accomplish in this life. I also hope that the little things I have accomplished— and hope to continue in the future—will end up helping others along the way. I strive to be able to make a positive difference in people's lives—even if it is just to a handful of people.

I've learned that one must learn to never lose the faith and the conviction that, in the end, it all works out somehow. It is important to remain perceptive and aware of the energy that surrounds us. I believe that love is energy and I've learned to perceive the energy of love everywhere—even when it takes me a while to recognize it.

I have made it my practice to allow nature's energy to embrace me slowly and nourish my soul. That energy makes me realize that we are never alone. I take the time to look at the ocean, the sun, the trees, the birds, and the flowers. It is there that I've found the most amazing answers throughout my life—especially during times when I had lost all hope.

I am convinced that you cannot fully understand what love really is unless someone has really loved you. It really doesn't matter who or where the love comes from. I also believe that, although we are here to love and help each other, there are those who will end up hurting us deeply. Rather than judging or reasoning why they act the way they do, it's best to stay away from individuals that have a negative emotional impact on our souls.

We must learn to appreciate the people in our lives who love us unselfishly—without reservation and without expecting anything in return—because that is the best kind of love.

Lastly, even when things don't go the way we planned,

it is best to keep a positive attitude because it is conducive to inner peace. That inner peace will eventually bring us closer to God.

I feel confident that this life is just a phase of a much bigger plan.

Acknowledgments

I want to express my sincere thanks to my Aunt Ofelia for encouraging me to finish writing this book.

About the Author

Born in Habana, Cuba. She came to the United States in 1970 at the age of fourteen. She has been living in the Unites States for forty years. Her unique life experiences, both in Cuba and in the United States, motivated and inspired her to write this book. She has been living with her family in New Jersey for the last twenty years.

www.ingramcontent.com/pod-product-compliance
Lightning Source LLC
Chambersburg PA
CBHW030353290526
45785CB00004B/1729